*A Promise of Change*

# A PROMISE OF CHANGE

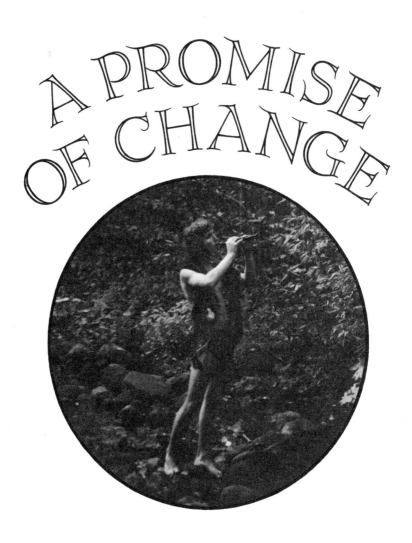

*Photography and text by*
### Walter Rinder

**CELESTIAL ARTS**
Millbrae, California

Celestial Arts
231 Adrian Road
Millbrae, California 94030

First Printing, September, 1979.

Made in the United States of America


**Library of Congress Cataloging in Publication Data**

Rinder, Walter.
    A promise of change.

    I.  Title.
PS3568.I5P7        811'.5'4        79-52161
ISBN 0-89087-269-4

     2   3   4   5   6   7 —   85   84   83   82   81   80

# Dedication...

*To my loving friend, David Stefan,*
*who once said to me,*
  *"Here there is*
    *no time,*
      *only life."*

*To my Gemini twin, Susie Brown,*
*who has given so much of herself*
*and has believed in me*
      *over the years . . .*

                *I love you both*

# 1

*You*
*are a person of value*
*in this world.*

*Your contribution is most important*
*for there are others,*
*not unlike yourself,*
*who desire your*
*knowledge,*
*the sharing of all your seasons,*
*your creative support,*

*and the knowing that there is a reliable and constant friendship.*

# 2

You
are a creature that
matters...

because you are a living energy,
with human touch that can heal
the ills of loneliness, the pain
of surrendering to fear, and the
guilt that sickens human endeavors,
crushing the limbs of human development.

*Your touch
is the mightiest recognition of
your loving energy.*

# 3

# Believe
## in your qualities...

*proudly,*
    *confidently.*

*Learn of your feelings,*
    *for they will instruct you toward*
    *your personal TRUTH*
        *and the KNOWING of*
        *universal truths*

*which bind all people
in a common peace,*

*a silent comfort,
a divine origin.*

Maintain faith
in the force that stirs
within you.

*It comes not from you*
*but moves through you.*

*Hurrying this energy*
*into relationships or accomplishments,*
*bringing maturity before its time,*
*is to taste the bitterness*
*of the unripened fruit*
*from the tree of experience.*

*Allow this force
to move at its own pace
in expanding the miracle
of your birth.*

*Let go
of all that is loved
and cherished
and beautiful in
your thoughts...*

rather than delight in the obsession of
possessing.

*For* to hold tightly
is to clip the wings of change
and change is the life-giving force
of free will
and personal independence.

*Only when love knows*
*it is free*
*will it express its nature.*

6

*Also
let go of all
that would restrain
or hold back...*

*your pursuit in cultivating*
*dreams,*
*aspirations,*
*and beliefs;*

*they are the heralds of your potential,*
*the kingdom of your imagination,*
*the succession of your reality.*

# 7

*Be compatible
with your sexuality.*

*Your nature gives it birth,*
*your sensitivity gives it direction,*
*your expression gives it maturity,*
*the comfort in which it lives outside you*
*will determine the quality of*
*your relationship to yourself.*

*Sexual expression is both an outpouring*
*of energy*
*and a rejuvenation,*
*a vital link to achieving*
*a healthy vision*
*when loving is your objective.*

# 8

*Speak to life
in the dialect you*

*are most familiar with...*

*as you gently,*
   *compassionately*
   *and directly search the simple nature*
      *of your mind and body.*

*Acknowledge life when it speaks to you.*

*It has much to tell you*
*from its timeless evolvement.*
*Honor the meaning of life,*
*through communication.*

# 9

*Be receptive*

*to another person's...*

*friendly personality;*
      *anticipate a dramatic addition.*

*If they see neither acceptance*
      *nor a response*
            *nor a caring spirit*
*they may withdraw*
            *inside themselves,*
            *shielding further action. . .*

*something is always lost*
*on these occasions,*
    *something withers and dies.*

# 10

*You are a kingdom*
*unto yourself...*

*No one can provide for your*
*happiness or security,*
*nor can they be given to you.*
*People can*
*contribute,*
*stimulate,*
*encourage,*
*increase*
*your happiness and security . . .*
*but you are their ultimate reality.*

*You* were born
        *the king*
        *of your inner world.*
*You* can fulfill your own needs
        *by understanding that*
        *you are in command of your future.*
*You* have no problems,
        *only choices and decisions.*
*Rule* your world
        *as a good leader,*
        *sharing happiness and security*
        *with those who enter your domain.*

# 11

# Retain
## a conscious state

*of inner balance...*

*as a worthwhile goal to achieve,*
*yet realize that it is not the arriving*
*that is your reward,*
*but the striving . . . .*

*We climb to the threshold of ourselves, in this, our earthly apprenticeship.*

# 12

# Promote and extend yourself...

in what you desire
your personality to be,
and choose your life's style and work
with every ounce of determination
you possess.
You have the divine right
to examine all facets of human
personalities and lifestyles
in deciding your own characteristics.

*If you allow others
to hinder the exploration
of your spirit,
to stifle your attempts
to know your depths,
you will forever suffer the slow death
of never knowing what
you might have been
or accomplished
with your life . . .
    a life so delicately given to you.*

# 13

*Revitalize your personal energy...*

*by channeling all kinds of loving
into your encounters and
acceptances . . .*

*to give is generous,*
*to receive is to surely gain;*
*not separating your giving and receiving*
*by gender,*
*or age,*
*or skin tone,*
*is to be in tune with your*
*natural innocence.*

# 14

*Appraise*
*your living* ...

*with your own standards of morality,*
*not with those counterfeited by others,*
*that you may become*
*a direct extension of your*
*Creator's morality.*

*All beliefs and actions lie*
*in the thinking you freely choose*
*to direct your journey.*
*This time called life*
*is NOW . . .*
*Choose your passage well.*

# 15

*Be vulnerable -
accept the hurts
and conflicts...*

*that may arise*
*from intimacy and experience.*
*To retreat from the closeness*
*that is inherent in caring for others*

*is to contaminate*
*the refreshment*
*that nourishes all living things.*

# 16

*Preserve your excitement and alertness...*

*for they are vital links to happiness*
*through human relationships,*
*conveying to all you meet,*

*the message that even though you may be*
*confronted with*
*rejection and*
*indifference,*
*your arteries will carry*
*truth through you,*
*as life rejoices in your presence.*

# 17

# Maintain a likeable attitude...

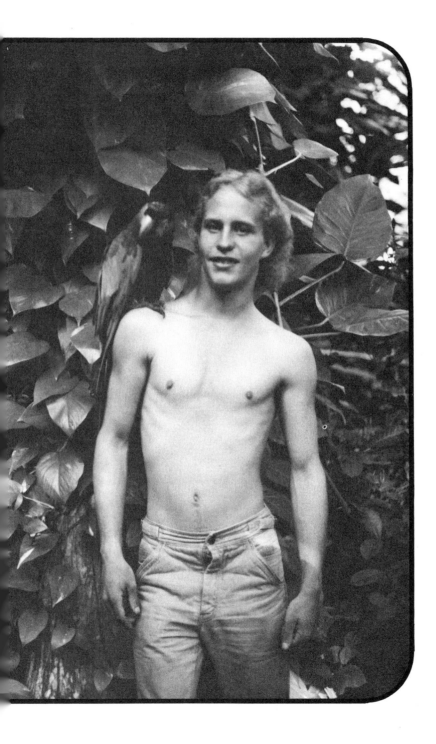

*by retaining a sincere friendship*
*with yourself.*

*Seek company to complement*
*your personality*
*and opposites who*
*attract your learning;*
*both are vital*
*in attaining successful character.*

*Loneliness and
isolation from love
are usually caused by
not letting people
know your needs,
your desires,
and the sparseness of
the expression of
your honest feelings.*

*A friendly appearance
will draw others to you.*

# 18

*Permit yourself time...*

*for your youthful exuberance,*
*to have fun*
*and become reacquainted*
*with life's playground.*

*We all need this*
*more than ever*
*because of the tension,*
*commitments,*
*responsibilities,*
*our society*
*requires of maturity.*

*This youth inside us all
softens the burdens,
allowing
curiosity and excitement
to accompany the
simple pleasures
that cannot be obtained
by monetary success.*

*The inferno of your thoughts can cause devastating destruction...*

*as your feelings and thinking
    battle to dominate your being.*

*Seek a truce
    whereby they can coexist
in a peaceful community of togetherness.*

*They originated from the same source; there was never any intent in separation or aggression.*

20

*Treat change as a*

*valuable friend...*

*who comes to you:*
  *not to take but to give of its wisdom,*
  *not to corrupt but to enhance,*
  *not to frighten but to encourage*
    *a greater depth to your*
  *understanding;*

*a promise of change*
  *builds archways for your thinking,*
    *entrances into*
  *the kingdom of love.*

## 21

Don't turn away from injustice or unfairness...

*either within your personal life*
*or the practices of society.*

*Any change or solution lies*
*in you . . .*
*as living proof of a just*
*and fair human being.*

*Intercept and protect truth as a child of innocence reaches out to you for assistance.*

*Look beyond*
*the apparent:*
*—what appears to be...*

*is many times only a*
*fragile shell holding*
*even more wonderment and*
*beauty inside.*

*See, perceive,*
*listen to the stillness.*

*When you can feel*
*the movement of all creation*
*in those instances,*
*you are in perfect knowing.*

# 23

*Treat death as
a necessary part
of life's design ...*

rather than dwelling upon the loss
through painful memories.

*N*o one has truly departed when
they are remembered by someone;
their life continues on
in the hearts of others and
through their influence on the
living.

*My father and friends
who have departed
live on
in my being because of
the loving we shared.*

*I am a better person because of their
guidance in my life's direction.*

*I will pass this on to others;
thus life's energy
continues.*

# 24

Be not afraid...
fear may enslave you

*in chill dungeons of insecurity,
exposing things unknown and
strange . . .*

*that they may wander in the warm glow of your reasoning and logic today, and your acceptance tomorrow.*

# 25

*Statements of feelings*
*such as promises and*
*"I love you"...*

*are words often gained easily*
*and too many times lost*
*in the murky fog*
*of forgetfulness.*

*Speak from your integrity*
*and the importance you place on your*
*remembering;*

*that life may witness*
*a wholesome birth*
*and a consistency in the*
*development of your statements* . . .

*today*
*and all the various tomorrows*
*of your sunny and cloud-filled days.*

# 26

*Always remember loving friendships cannot be owned,*

*controlled or abused by need,*
*    yet you can become the caretaker*
*        of love's home*
*and the grounds of honor and honesty*
*        that surround it.*

*It is not the need
for loving friendship
that is praised
but in the sharing
that our joy
is enriched.*

27

*Be comfortable with*

*your differentness...*

*you have the right*
    *to experience yourself*
    *by your own values and standards.*

*Who recognizes you*
    *better than yourself?*

*. . . except for those rare few, who are*
    *truth-seekers*
        *themselves,*
    *who support and encourage you.*

*D*on't be a copy.
*B*e an original.
*T*hey're more valuable.

*You deserve to be in an environment...*

*where there is a feeling of*
*belonging,*
*where you can play,*
*where you can work,*
*where you can create,*

*and practice active participation*
*in being*
*yourself*
*without interference,*
*ridicule,*
*condemnation,*
*intimidation.*

*You*
*are a person of value*
*in this world ...*

*don't run away from your spirit;*
*walk to it confidently.*

*Life*

*is awaiting the arrival*
*of all your potential.*

*Life is waiting
to applaud
your performance.*

You are a
creation of love.
You are a
creator of loving.

*You,
my new friend,
are the
Promise of
Change!*

*Photo by Jonivan*

*I have discovered that wisdom must be a living activity, not an intellectual dialogue. The simple and the innocent people seem to live closer to a life of wise understanding than the rich, or the learned, or the influential.*

*We too often make commitments and promises to other people, dismissing the importance of promises made to ourselves concerning personal development and well-being.*

*Living wisdom . . . realizing our values and changing is what this book represents.*

*If you would like to share your feelings with me, please write to me:*

*Walter Rinder*
*c/o Celestial Arts*
*231 Adrian Rd.*
*Millbrae, California 94030*

## OTHER BOOKS BY WALTER RINDER

FRIENDS AND LOVERS is a joyful exploration through words and photographs of the power of loving relationships to bring personal meaning and renewal to life. In the tradition of the best-selling LOVE IS AN ATTITUDE. 128 pages, soft cover, $5.95

FOLLOW YOUR HEART is one of Walter Rinder's most popular works in a newly revised edition. His universal appeal has made him a publishing phenomenon. Beautiful photographs by the author. 64 pages, soft cover, $3.95

In LOVE IS AN ATTITUDE, Walter Rinder is "a gently compassionate artist. . . a man who recognizes the source of beauty that love and understanding engender and who urges us to find it. Rinder is also an artist, blending his photos to text happily."—*Peninsula Living*. 128 pages, soft cover, $5.95

AURA OF LOVE uses gentle, sensitive words and illustrations to celebrate the little-understood value of self-image in love. Rinder bears joyful witness to the feelings of self-worth and the freedom to give to another that emanate from a love of self. 64 pages, soft cover, $3.95

THIS TIME CALLED LIFE is "such a completely beautiful book. . . here is writing of the highest quality illustrated by remarkable photographs of nature and people." —*Los Angeles Times*. 160 pages, soft cover, $5.95

In WILL YOU SHARE WITH ME? Walter Rinder shares his love and desires, fulfilled and unfulfilled. Sensitively illustrated with his own photographs. 128 pages, soft cover, $5.95

LOVE IS MY REASON is a positive approach to life and love in which Walter Rinder speaks of our vast human potential. 128 pages, soft cover, $5.95

In WHERE WILL I BE TOMORROW? Walter Rinder combines prose, poetry and eloquent photography to tell of the love of a man for another man. 144 pages, soft cover, $5.95

Walter Rinder's books are available at your local book or department store or directly from the publisher. To order by mail, send check or money order to:

CELESTIAL ARTS
231 Adrian Road
Millbrae, California 94030

Please include $1.00 for postage and handling. California residents add 6% sales tax.